G

Island Folklore and More

Leslie Stewart

ISBN 978-0-9866065-3-3

Additional copies or permissions are obtained from the author:
    Mr. Leslie Stewart
    831 Cambridge Road RR 2
    Montague, PE C0A 1R0
    Canada

Other information is available from the publisher:
    Wood Island Prints
    670 Trans-Canada Highway, RR 1
    Belle River, PE C0A 1B0
    Canada
    (902) 962-3335
    schultz@pei.sympatico.ca

Printing and binding by:
    Lightning Source Inc. (US)
    1246 Heil Quaker Blvd.
    La Vergne, TN 37086 USA
    Voice: (615 213-5815
    Fax: (615) 213-4725
    Email: inquiry@lightningsource.com
    www.lightningsource.com

Thanks to my wife, Dorrie, for going through the proof and fixing more of my creative spelling.

Introduction

This is my fourth book of stories and island poems and I'm sure you will enjoy this book much like you did the others, that is if you read the books.

Maybe you bought them for a friend or a relative, one that you love and respect beyond all others. This book, *GO'WAY! Island Folklore and More,* provides more of the island humour and sadness that invokes our everyday life on the red island. Our island, that's floating peacefully in the Gulf of St Lawrence. Some days we are closer to the mainland, as our island grows with the low tides and shrinks with the overbearing power of the high tides increasing the distance between the mainland and ourselves. There is talk of a bridge to be built between New Brunswick and the island—these are stories not to be taken seriously, and my stories are more realistic. Take the poem *Spot* for instance.

Table of Contents

Table of Contents

Beach Scum

Tracy went a walkin'
Along the island shore
Now what on the beach
Was she a lookin' for?

It couldn't be that man
She had thrown from the house
I remember her a sayin'
He was nothin' but a louse

She flipped over some stones
And fumbled through the weeds
Tracy was a lookin' for something
No doubt she doesn't need

She was lonely and very mad
Looked ever quite depressed
As she walked along the beach
In her white weddin' dress

Blood a boilin' in her veins
Then she came upon another
She looked up at this woman
Who was pregnant as a mother?

They gave a nod in respect
As they walked along the way
She to be dressed for a wedding
On this occasion, her special day

Then beneath a pile of seaweed
Of driftwood and ocean slime
Tracy found her man
As the other said "He's mine"

Sure as it can be, it happened
On that heart- broken shore
The two women buried the scum
Who shall marry vow no more
Who shall marry vow no more.

Old Cape Light

I pause at my restaurant table
Only, to marvel at this view
Of the reflecting Cardigan River
The Cape windows I look through

I see fishing boats painted white
And many pleasure craft I see
Then this one magnificent sailboat
With crew are heading out to sea

The sea breeze was fresh to my face
As the morning sun warmed up the day
I sit drinking my fresh brewed coffee
This view is priceless I would say

I dream of tall ships full of sail
Built here on the historic Cardigan shore
Real adventures of seafaring men
The island life of the rich and poor

But today I sit at my restaurant table
Looking through the windows: a delight
Dreaming of those years gone by
While eating at Old Cape Light

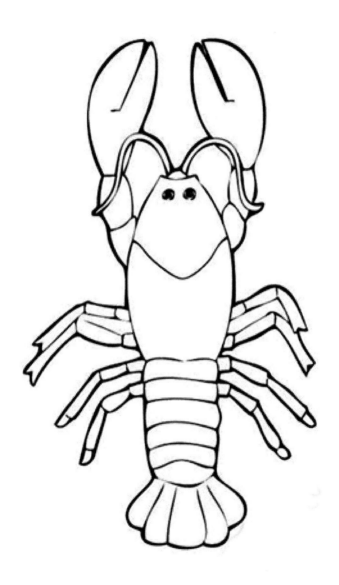

Martha

Martha brings me coffee
Martha brings her a tea
Martha brings the menu
And she does it happily

Martha brings more coffee
Martha brings more tea
How would like your breakfast,
Dorrie and Leslie?

Martha brings our breakfast
Martha, this is such a good deal
When dining at Cape Light
You'll enjoy a delicious meal

We always come for coffee
We always come for tea
Often we bring our friends
Or even some family

Martha brought more coffee
Martha brought more tea
Martha brought the bill
And she did it happily

I Plum Did It

There are plenty of stories
Of boys climbing trees
Well this here is another
Story that involves me

We lived out in the country
Not too far from a lane
Where some plum trees grew
Yellow ones all the same

The trees grew close together
Difficult to climb for a plum
They had many little branches
You could only climb on some

We would head out across
The field and down the lane
Cross the stream on the bridge
The plum trees were the game

Sometimes we would use an
Old broken hockey stick
A baseball bat or pole
Those trees were some thick

This one time I remember
Oh so very, very well
I was up in the plum trees
Below was my sister Mel

For some unknown reason
I can't explain to this day
I was up in the plum tree
With a knife, swinging away

Not a little knife it was
But a large kitchen knife
Swinging at the plums
Holding on for dear life

The knife slipped from my hand
Falling down towards the ground
At that same time my sister
Had moved, her head it found

Yes I see that strange scene
As my knife, stuck in her head
My little sister Melinda, running
Arms flailing, the words she said

They where bad words all right
Mostly I remember her running away
She looked like a chicken in flight
There was some bleeding; she was ok

I asked Melinda about this story
On a visit not so long ago
She said she didn't remember it
But if I'm telling it, it must be so

Fathers Day Paddle

I was telling some of my
Friends the other day
It was my dear Dad who
Taught me how to canoe

I had always sat on the bottom
Or in the middle of the canoe
My mom paddled from the bow
Dad guided the stern, he knew how

It was a week before Fathers Day
Dad was cutting a small pine board
Into a small canoe paddle just for me
I can help cut and sand it, Daddy

A week later on June thirteenth
My paddle well coated in varnish
We headed down to St Mary's Bay
This would be the best Fathers Day

This would be my first time
In the canoe as a crew member
Excitement of adventure me and Dad
With my new paddle I was so glad

A new life jacket of bright yellow
A gift for me from my mom
I looked like a large bumble bee
Buzz, buzz, Hey Dad look at me

I sat proudly at the front of our
Family's 16 foot fibreglass dream
Listening to every word he knew
About paddling the green canoe

My father pushed the canoe into
St. Mary's Bay; away we went
With my small paddle, I took a stroke
It made a creaking sound, then broke

I could feel those tears running
Over my nose down my face
My Dad saw and felt my pain
Take my paddle and try again

At the stern of the canoe sat Dad
On this, his Father of Father's Day
With the spare weathered paddle of time
Beside him the broken paddle of mine

Fire Ball

I just went to stand beside the fire,
Suddenly the flames shot me higher.
It seems I had passed some bad gas,
I went through the roof, landing on the grass.

No doubt I had a shocked expression!
Landing on the ground, leaving an impression!
I left a hole, just the size of my head,
Impact as this, I should've been dead.

I responded quite well in spite of it all.
Rising to my feet, I didn't seem as tall!
The impact it seems shorten me some,
It would've been better, to land on my bum.

Now we would have to fix the hole in the roof.
The shine I'd had? Must have been a 100 proof?
I called our neighbour, to give us a hand.
We would have to fix it, the best we can.

When he arrived, laughing and full of cheer,
He couldn't believe my story; I said "Look here."
There was a hole to the night sky, stars shining bright,
We all stood in the kitchen, looking into the night.

He thought I was joking about the fiery ride.
To be shot, as if from a cannon from inside!
Plain to see the burned hole in my jeans,
My poor scorched bum was easily seen.

He studied my bum, then looked at the roof,
You were drinking that old shine? 100 proof?
I said, "I was" and standing beside the stove.
Had passed some bad gas, the flames shot me so.

He continued to laugh and dance around,
I told him, I was shorter after hitting the ground.
This was way too much; he stood there and laughed,
He bend over so much, suddenly he passed gas!

A ball of fire, as a rocket leaving a pad,
He lifted through the roof much as I had.
Through the night sky, leaving a fiery trail,
Good thing for us! He left no smell!

We looked at each other, not believing our eyes,
There goes our neighbour, into the night sky.
It was the last time we ever saw him! I say.
As he shot through the night sky, on his way!

When we see a comet or a falling star?
We're ever so thankful, where we are?
I'm shorter then I was, but two feet on the ground.
He left Prince Edward Island! Never to be found.

Bottle-man

Bottle – man, bottle- man, who can be that bottle- man

Rides his bike, most every day,
Pick-en up bottles, gone a-stray
Most people lose them from their car
Open windows, they can throw them far.

It's a good thing, he has a bike,
Way too far for the old guy to hike.
Wears a helmet and a safety vest to,
This old guy cleans up, for me and you

I've seen him working in early morn,
Then once we saw him, in a thunderstorm.
Lighting didn't hit him, he was doing all right
Did you ever see the bottle picker's bike?

Bottle-man, bottle-man, who can be that bottle-man

Pick-en up pop bottles, beer one too,
Can it be bud, Canadian or blue?
Short stubby bottles, they got no neck,
He picks them up, saying what the hick

If you're ever over Montague way,
You just might see him working that day.
Loads his bike, to the depot he goes,
Recycles those bottles for a million or so

People drive by, their kids will say
He picks up bottles gone a-stray
There may not be much time for him,
Those bottles soon may turn to tin,

Bottle-man, bottle-man, who can be that bottle-man

Dedicated to Melvin Blaisdell

Tir Na Nog

I went to a Halloween party
And wore my red plaid skirt
Had on my matching tam hat
Along with an ancient shirt

Strolled into the parlour room
Weird creatures everywhere
I didn't see this one old witch
Who was sitting on a chair

Halloween really scares me
Partying at Tir Na Nog

She put her leg up under my skirt
And then tried to lift it high
Curiosity had gotten into the witch
Was I a woman or a guy?

I was saved by this religious one
He wore a dress something like mine
This blessed old fellow lent a hand
Protecting my bare behind

Halloween really scares me
Partying at Tir Na Nog

I saw our host preparing the food
"Will" was setting the table top
With some turkey, ham and salad bar
Welcoming us to their party was "Dot"

I took my glass of vintage wine
And strolled about their house
In another room other strangers sat
They were all to quiet as a mouse

Halloween really scares me
Partying at Tir Na Nog

Lift your glasses, I said to them
It doesn't matter if it's wine or beer
This is a Halloween party you're at
So tilt your glasses and party here

I heard their chatter as I turned away
Went into a room with a table round
Sat with the Pope, a Vampire, a Pirate
Then this talking Lamp Shade I found

Halloween really scares me
Partying at Tir Na Nog

We talked about life on the other side
The lamp said he wasn't all that bright
And Dracula downed a pint of blood
Said to myself this will be a hell of a night

Had a conversation with a Gingerbread Man
Said she was conceived on a cookie tin
The question was answered for all of us
This explains why you're so thin

They welcomed party goers to Tir Na Nog
Will, Brandon and Dot did say
We thank you all for coming tonight
But in our home you can't stay

Halloween used to scare me
When partying at Tir Na Nog

Les in a Dress

Halloween

Halloween, Halloween
Scariest of all nights it seems
There are hairy things
There are scary things
All of witch scare me

Ghosts and goblins come
Mummies dressed for fun
Little witches and cats
Jack -o -lanterns, vampire bats
They all scare poor me

Some dress as super stars
Or spacemen from afar
Men dress in ladies wear
With wigs of neon hair
They really scare me

I see doctors and a nurse
Another guy drives a hearse
I see a pumpkin in a coffin
Now you don't see that often
But it did scare me

Little children come to call
I like these creatures best of all
I give out candy for a treat
It rots their teeth when they eat
Boy does Halloween scare me

Blood-sucking Les

What the Hal

We know this man
From Gaspereaux
Hal Jamieson is
The man we know

He's not afraid
Of ice and snow
Into the frigid
Waters he goes

Hal goes swimming
On New Years Day
Runs through the
Frozen ocean spray

Icicles dripping
From his brow
Damn that water
Must be cold, Hal

Panmure Island is
His swimming ground
On New Years Day
Hal can be found

Polar Bear swimming
For an icy dip
Better be careful
Hal, you don't slip

He's braver than
I'll ever be
Taking a swim
In the frozen sea

Is he crazy?
Or just insane
Hal Jamieson
Is his name

Salt Water Sam   10

Salt Water Sam
Is a hell of a man
Doing what he can

Instead of making moonshine
He'd try making homemade wine
An Island drink of a different kind

Driving along at Guernsey Cove
He noticed a vineyard as he drove
Almost stopped going so slow

There in a field before his eyes
Grew some grapes he could try
Cheaper to take some, than to buy

Had some old fish boxes in the truck
Old Sam couldn't believe his luck
Behind the grape vines he did duck

Filled the boxes full of grapes
Then heard a rig, had better wait
Before he dragged them to the gate

Truck was loaded headed for home
Called his buddy on the cell phone
Got to stomp some grapes, can't do it alone

Into the house and they filled the tub
Salt Water Sam and his bud
They stomped about rub-a-dub-dub

They had forgotten to plug the drain
All that work had been in vain
But those two men never complained

That was the end of making wine
Sam will try a brew of a different kind
Then he saw a pasture of dandelions

Swim like a Fish

I was testing the water
Not thinking of going in
I don't why I did that
Because I can't swim

It did look inviting
Clean, warm and blue
And the refection of
Someone that I knew

Then the voice of reason
Rippled from the water
Don't be afraid, Dad
The voice of my daughter

It will be alright Dad
Trust me I can swim
At that precise moment
My daughter pushed me in

With my arms flailing
My legs splashing about
Spitting out blue water
I managed to shout

Help me? Help me? This isn't funny
As I bob up and down
This is a helluva way to go
Pushed in a pool to drown

But Dad, comes that voice
Of my daughter on the side
Do you not remember?
Throwing me in, I cried

Now I'm not getting even
Heck no, I'm not mad
That as a little helpless girl
You threw me in, bad Dad

You will have to swim
Just swim like a fish
I remember you to say
As you did, I made this wish

That someday, I'll get even
And now that time has come
Swim like a fish, dear Father
Throwing me in wasn't fun

Just tell your Father to stand
The pool is not that deep
Watching your Dad drown
Is giving me the creeps

It was true just as they said
As I stood up in water to my chin
Rebecca had got even with me
For throwing my little girl in

I wonder if she remembers
When I stuck her with that pin
Putting on a clean cloth diaper
It'll be worse than learning to swim

Clay Road to Heaven

Clay road to heaven
Clay road too far
As I walk that road
I'll find where you are

It's a lonely road
That leads me to you
I've been walking alone
It's what I must do

You left me so many
Now long years ago
We had our first kiss
At the old fishing hole

It was on that dusty
Red island clay road
Our lives changed
Forever, I've been told

We walked hand in hand
Fishing poles in the other
Along driving a truck
Came your dear mother

In my ragged blue jeans
Barefoot and knobbly knees
Your enraged dear mother
Drove her truck into me

I left your loving and
So young held hand
I was thrown in the air
Into a tree I did land

Dead as a door knob
Snuffed out as a candle
Dust in the wind
A pot without a handle

Yes, and I still walk
These red clay roads
This journey will end
When we meet I'm told

So many fishing holes
And young people I see
They're falling in love
Same as you and me

At the end of the road
Your old image I see
I have one burning question
Why did your mother hit me?

Clay road to heaven
Clay road not my luck
As we walked that road
Hit by your mothers truck

Beach Treasure

I've sold my island soul
For a better way of life
Gone over to the mainland
To find myself a wife

The red shores of home
Drift there in my mind
I had wandered the shore
For a wife I didn't find

Lots of broken traps
Sea weed to sea glass
Mussel buoys to shells
Flip flops to old trash

No valued buried treasures
Stranded mermaids on shore
Some fifty years of looking
Now I would look no more

In frustration and pain
I had given up all hope
I will leave my island
In my old wooden boat

Then bad luck to worse
Caught in a sudden gale
If I drown will it be
Go to heaven or hell?

My old wooden row boat
Drifted with the wild sea
Smashed upon some rocks
On what shore can this be?

Like all sea junk that is
Washed up, upon a shore
I was found by a stranger
Who was looking for more

Covered in slimy sea weed
Clinging to a broken oar
I was found as a treasure
Washed up, upon her shore

I thanked the good Lord
For saving my poor life
He could have done better
In finding me that wife

The first words I said
Were "Yes I do"
Now we're married
No thanks to you

I'm busy building myself
Another wooden row boat

Captain Charlotte

Charlotte's dead man's chest
Is at the bottom of a harbour
Buried in mud, silt and rock
This its final hidden place of rest

A pirates King's ransom in gold
Adding to it diamonds, silver
Rubies, emeralds and sapphires
This is how the story is told

The dreaded Captain Charlotte
Sailed these muddy island shores
Looking for a special burial place
He was in luck and found this spot

At the mouth of a special river
The Hillsborough be its name
Into waters of fresh and ocean salt
His pirate's chest he did deliver

Now unfortunately for the crew
The Captain he killed them all
One by one he did the deed
The location only he now knew

He sank the burning pirate ship
Sending it to a muddy grave
He then rowed safely to shore
On a mossy covered stone slipped

Cutting open a hole in his bald head
Causing him to lose all memory
He was now lost wandering the shore
Confused, tired and now almost dead

No memory of the slaughtered men
Nor that of the sunken ship and chest
Days turned into weeks then months
When finally he was found by a friend

Another old pirate of days gone by
Knew Captain Charlotte very well
They had crewed together once
It was Charlotte had put out his eye

Patch be Nimble was his name
A cut-throat of a bastard pirate
Knew the captain had a treasure
But where she be was the game

No ship, no crew, no treasure
They poured hot rum inside him
Trying to make him talk or mumble
Rambling stories they took measure

Winter was coming on too fast
It was find the treasure now
Or leave it for the next spring
Captain Charlotte wouldn't last

Patch be Nimble lost his wit
Lashing out at the Captain
With his sword in hand
Our captain's neck he did hit

It was off with his head indeed
No more looking for treasure clues
The mystery was gone and parted
And no more, wasted hot rum to feed

Patch be Nimble's crew departed
The shore and Charlotte's head
Leaving old stories to be told
And new waters now charted

A marker was made on the ground
That read "Here lays a cruel pirate
Killed his crew and sank his ship
A headless Captain Charlotte found."

Others came to explore these grounds
Of the mighty Hillsborough River
A harbour safe from storms and sea
A place we now call Charlottetown

At night on shore as the sun goes down
You can hear screams of sailors' souls
Watch for the burning ship at sunset
Feel the chill of death as it's all around

Now remember all that was said
A pirate's life was meant to be fun
Drinking rum and party at sea
Best remember not to lose your head

Image

As I was strolling passed this window?
There was this face I didn't know
It did have some familiar features
This odd, but handsome creature

His head of wild Hieland grey
A mob of hair on this windy day
It had a strange likeness to seaweed
As it moved with the wind indeed

I could see the aged lines of time
They are a roadmap of life we find
No doubt as a baby this face was smooth
But it shows, it has been very will used

Hard to measure the age of his face
No younger than fifty in any case
Sixty five, maybe again a tad high
For he is still a handsome guy

He doesn't display much of a tan
No doubt an inside worker this man
Perhaps a fish plant worker he might
Just sleeps all day and works at night

His choice of colourful clothes I admire
Nice yellow shirt, his pants could be higher
That pot belly rest on his belt buckle
Much as it did on my wife's uncle

I'll just tuck in my shirt, as not to be like him
For I take pride in myself, am tall and slim
I feel as if I'm starting to know this guy
For what reason, I really don't know why

Maybe I'll give a friendly nod his way
He might just think of me another day
Why he did just the same to me
Must have thought I was a she

Better check my watch, yes time is near
Late for dinner and best be out of here
He's leaving too, what chance can that be
As I passed the window, I was looking at me

Love Lost

I haven't seen you in a long time
I thought you were my friend.
I haven't seen you in a long time
Will I ever see you again?

I still think of us together,
My darling island Heather.
We were young children playing
I remember, both of us saying.

No matter were we went in life,
To be together, really would be nice.
We were young children falling in love
We would be like, those mourning doves.

We could travel to the lovely places together,
And be together as one, for ever and ever.
They were only pictures in our school books,
Do you remember? We dreamed as we looked.

You held my hand coming home from school,
I should have kissed you then, what a fool.
That was silly of me to think that way
Because? I was going to marry you someday.

School ended and summer came alive.
We spent our days together you and I.
Climbing trees, running through the daisies,
My mom said, "We were two young crazies."

If we were playing, at your house or mine,
We were having a wonderful summertime.
Digging for clams, red clay oozing between our toes,
Your dad would say, "Be careful, clams bite you know."

Your mom said, "We should all go for a swim."
We went down to the beach at Point Prim.
I will always remember that sad day,
It was in August, the eighth, a Sunday.

We had just come in from our swim.
The summer sun was drying our salty skin.
Sitting on the red clay bank, looking out to sea,
You put your soft hand in mine, and looked at me.

We are moving away, my father told us.
No work on the island, so leave we must.
He might get a job working in some car plant,
We're moving to Ontario, staying with my Aunt.

My heart sank as a boat in stormy seas.
When are you moving? When will it be?
It's Friday the thirteenth, father told my mom.
That's this Friday, But why? How come?

The fish plant is shutting down.
They say not enough lobsters around.
It was a poor spring, prices were too low.
I don't understand, that's all I know!

I was not at the ferry dock that sad day.
It would've hurt too much, so I stayed away.
I did ride my bike, down to the banks of Little Sands.
And watched as the ferry, took you away from my island.

I know we were young, and knew nothing about love.
I also knew we would never be like those mourning doves.
We would never sit, and hold each others hand.
No more would I be summer crazy, on the island.

If you wrote a letter, it never got to me.
My mother would say, "Just wait and see."
Nothing ever came; you just vanished away.
Yet, I still think of you each passing day.

I am now an old islander, sitting down at Point Prim.
I sit on that bank, remembering our last swim.
When Old Home Week comes, I go into town.
I'm hoping to see you there, as I look around.

I look at the attractive women on the street.
And pray to God, we might some day meet.
I would like to do that before I die.
This old man now sits, about to cry.

I wonder if I had kissed you that day?
Would I still be in love this way?
There is a sharp pain now in my chest.
I better lie down now, and take that rest.

I haven't seen you in a long time.
Will I ever see you again?

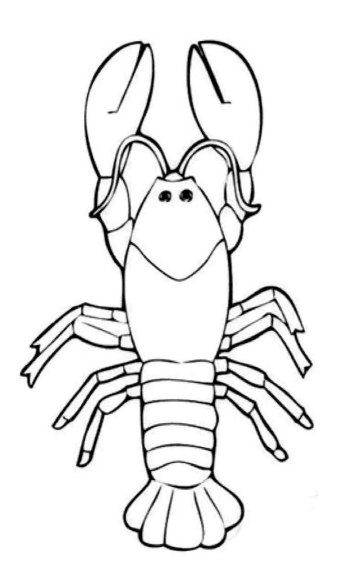

School Days

It has been ever so long
As a child going to school
I sat there staring at you
Many times I felt the fool

Other boys bought you gifts
Flowers, bubble gum, candy bars
A pen or pencil or an eraser
Once you got a frog in a jar

I never gave you anything
Too shy, I didn't have a chance
Saw Bobby pull your ponytail
That was his way of romance

I studied and barely passed
Each year harder than before
When finally in grade eight
I quit and walked out the door

From a distance in town
I watched as you grew
You went to high school
As for me, you never knew

Sometimes there would be a party
In a friend of a friend's house
I might find that opportunity
To be near you, quiet as a mouse

Listening to your soft voice
Maybe breathe a weft of perfume
Never lingering on my stay
You never saw me, I presume

Later we worked at the local
Red and White food store
You worked the front cash
And I cleaned all the floors

We spent our time at the store
Passing each other in the aisle
And every now and then
You gave me a nice smile

After a couple of short years
You took your mother's advice
Time to leave Murray River
And start a new, better life

I remained cleaning floors
And stacking all the shelves
In the wintertime cleaning
Sidewalks and playing an elf

If I had a Christmas wish
From old Santa it would be
You were back at the River
Working at the store with me

That wish never happened
The store—it closed down
I moved to live in Montague
And a new better job I found

Cleaning the floors and windows
In the beautiful Down East Mall
Some of my old teachers pass by
Say they're surprised I found a job at all

This is a grand place to work
As most people shop here I say
I overheard this conversation
You were coming home to stay

Some ten years have passed by
Since the last time I saw your face
You had gone west to a University
Seems you left without a trace

I heard stories some people told
But they were only jealous of you
You had done the right thing
Leaving the island, it was best to do

So I waited for your arrival
Just a curious thing I might say
That in a couple of more weeks
You'll be in Murray River to stay

I thought of those many years past
Of dreaming and worshiping you
My thoughts had held me together
Over these long lonely years like glue

That all dissolved in rapid time
A good thing the mall doors are wide
Her five dirty kids must have pushed
Some awful hard to get all of her inside

They say she had gone out west
To expand her learning mind
I see now all that expanded
Was her getting a large behind?

This was not my dream girl
Of school days and Red and White
My good Lord, I may never sleep
Erasing dreams, of her those nights

The Other Side

The other side was always a mystery to me
I had often heard this phrase when smaller.
Now you all know to a youngster
Almost everything in life seems taller.

I mean people were tall, horses, trees
Barns, and our house was a castle.
I grew up with one sister and two brothers
My grandma, my parents—what a hassle

I never saw a real castle, only in pictures
But my dad always said, "He was the king"
The entire island was his Sherwood Forest
Visitors from the other side, gifts they bring

One time standing in MacGreedy's general store
Standing beside my Grandma holding her hand
I heard mister MacGreedy telling my Grandma
Great gifts, all things come from the mainland

Now hearing of this only confused me more
Was the mainland the other side?
From our tiny house on the island shore
You could see it; only in the fog did it hide

What was this big deal about the other side?
If I could see it with my tiny eyes
Standing on the shore gazing away
The other side, if it was, was large in size

Remember when one is small things do look bigger
The other side must be a marvellous place to be
It seems most families bought their thing from there
My Grandma said, "The best things come from the sea"

The other side was bigger than I could imagine
Not only does it make things, it can lose things too
Shopping with my mom and sister at the post office
At MacGreedy's store, he asked my mom, "What could he do"

The parcel she had ordered last month, hadn't come
She did have a card however saying it was lost in the mail
Mother asked him to take a look in the store for the parcel
Mister MacGreedy said, "It was not lost in his store, he could tell"

"The parcel it seems had been sent back by mistake
And was now lost somewhere on the other side", said he
We all looked at each other with our own lost expressions
To lose a parcel, one so valuable, how can that be?

No one in our family had ever left the island
It had never come up as something we might do
There were so many places on the island we hadn't seen
Like Charlottetown or Summerside we hadn't gone to

The thought of the other side, lost as in the mail
I had bad dreams for a week, thinking about that
As a boy wandering the faraway shores
Lost in some forest not knowing were I was at

I will wait my time and learn more about things
Already the mystery has doubled, to two sides
I have learned there is land on the other side of the island
Are there two mainlands? Two places from the other side?

A place they call Borden, a place we have never been
They say lies a different other side to us
There is a bridge you can take to the other side
No doubt this is a tall story, in it I don't trust

I will wait for another day to see if this is right
There is so much ahead of me, others will show me how
As for right now, just being a child is enough
I'm looking forward to the other side, just not now

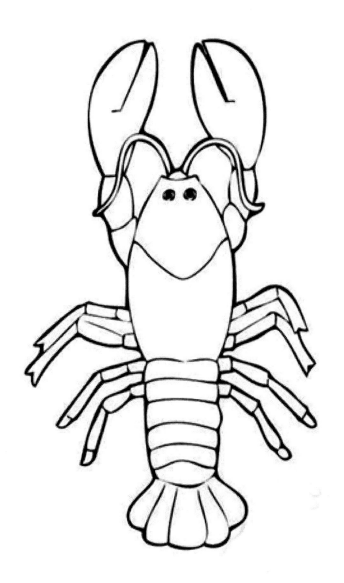

Angel in a bottle

I need an angel
This morning!
I need an angel all right
I slept with the devil
Again last night

Oh, he was hot
And horny as hell
My good God!
His breath did smell

This was my last
Night's sleep with him
I'm going to drink wine
Give up on that gin

Another bad night alone
Like a dog in the ghetto
Demons in my dreams
Love torturing me so

If I had an angel
To sleep with at night
I'd hold that smooth
Bottle, close and tight

I've tried the rum brothers
One dark, the other white
They kept me from sleeping
We wrestled all the night

From laughter to tears
Even a suicidal thought
With these two brothers
Drinking, fun it was not

I found me another
A lover called Amaretto
When I consume his love
My stomach is full

A bottle of Southern Comfort
I was a hippy for a day
I just need that angel
One to show me the way

Looking far into the spirit
I soon found a Russian spy
He was clear to see through
Smirnoff Vodka, is the guy

But it's the future I see
Looking into an empty glass
The refection of a drunk
I've been nothing but an ass

Slept with that old Devil
A smooth hot bottle is he
His fiery breath smells
Engulfing me internally

I need an angel this morning
I need an angel all right
I need the good Lord
To show me the light

Sleepy Hollow

A hotel of great charm
An architectural design
This fine hotel is home
To those that like crime

The court will give you
A pass for the clerk
When you arrive here
It's welcome home, jerk

They'll find you a friend
One to share the night
In this tiny little cell
Have fun, sleep tight

We hope to make your stay
As enjoyable as we can
While you serve your time
In the Sleepy Hollow Pen

The room rates aren't cheap
You'll pay a hefty price
This is where some people go
Those who haven't been nice

It has its own special reputation
As the one in New York State
We have our own wild horsemen
That will help and incarcerate

It's their job to find you
And they do it so well
Take a look around you
At your buddies in jail

Leslie Stewart: Go'Way!

Enjoy your holidays here
You have plenty of time
To wonder why you had
To commit those crimes

Welcome to Sleepy Hollow
Hotel to the criminal kind
You'll have an awesome holiday
While serving your time

Mind over Matter

I've lost the things
That I can't find
I'm beginning to
Lose my mind

Was it in the closet?
Or in the basement below
Maybe stored in the attic
Where it is I don't know

I may have left it in
The trunk of the car
Along with the other stuff
Wonder where the keys are

Last time lobster fishing
Might have lost it in the bay
When was I fishing last?
Was it last year or yesterday?

With all this junk scattered
In the house or on the ground
It makes it difficult to find
The things that aren't around

I will ask my dear wife
To help and take a look
Can't remember her name
I'll go and ask the cook

He said we were not married
And what kind of a man was I
Thought I was married once
But I guess not to this guy

Things are getting harder
For me to try and find
There is no question now
I have really lost my mind

Chest Pains

I just got this awful pain
Running through my chest

It drove me to the ground
One of life's horrible tests

I had eaten the wrong foods
Never enjoyed what was best

Lots of French fries and gravy
Greasy foods I can't digest

I'm just slightly overweight
Ran a gravel truck out west

Back home on the island
Taking a well-deserved rest

I hadn't expected this so soon
Just had a heart and lung test

I am waiting for the results
Before changing for the best

What an awful pain this is
Running through my chest

My arms have now gone numb
Face down on the floor I'll rest

This is a hell of a way to go
Better eating habits I guess

This casino floor is cold
But I'm sweating here at best

The light is at the end of my day
Dying of a heart attack more or less

The pain is now gone away inside
Dead now taking that long, long rest

Leslie Stewart: Go'Way!

Heavenly Ash

Grey was the day
Darker was the night
Unable to see
The sun's bright light

Volcanic floating ash
Lands upon the ground
Travelling is difficult
To see, move around

Wearing mask to breathe
Filtering choking air
Falling volcanic ash
Landing everywhere

Crops are ruined
Livestock are dying
We'll try to survive
No tears for crying

Jet air currents
Blowing this way
Bring the deadly ash
Burying all today

Those with boats
Their families flee
Take their chances
In stormy seas

They'll be unable
To see or navigate
Take their chances
Death or to escape

Once, Red Island shores
Succumb to volcanic ash
Suffocating our last breath
Our lives have now past

What had we done
To deserve this fate?

Saltwater Sam   11

Saltwater Sam
Is a hell of a man
Doing the best he can

Sam bought himself a plough
To move all that snow somehow
Can't wait for another storm do it now

He pushed and pulled in vain
Trying to clear his long lane
His back and legs were in pain

He hooked the plough to his pickup truck
But this brought him no luck
The old truck was forever stuck

He had no chains for his tires
So used some old barbed wire
He was ready now to try her

Still no better for traction
But his neighbour liked the action
Watching Sam and his contraption

The lane was long full of snow
But his ploughing device wouldn't go
It was just his bad luck, you know

His neighbour came to lend a hand
To help his good neighbour, Sam
This plough isn't for snow but the land

Sam had got the wrong kind of plough
This one won't move snow no how
It's for turning over the land some how

Forget the lane and ploughing the snow
I'll bring over my tractor and blow
The lane clear, I'm a neighbour, you know

Store Bought Card

I gave my father a gift
On this his Father's Day
A store bought card with
A message I couldn't say

How do I say I love you?
In my arms hold you tight
Look deep into your eyes
And say that you were right

Take your wrinkled hand
Go outside for a walk
We never had conversations
I don't think we ever talked

I was so afraid when small
Trouble surrounded our life
Your drinking, and swearing
Beatings—they weren't nice

I was always late coming home
It was better to freeze in the night
Stand on a lonely street corner
Than to come finding a fight

My older brothers and sisters
Were quick to leave our home
Each one on their own way
Hoping for a better life alone

In their search to find happiness
That would bring them love
Most tripped up on their search
For that elusive mourning dove

They seem to have it on track now
Raising children of their own
Some of them drank like you
At first they had broken homes

Now they have come to realize
What a wasted life it could be
They too have the same problem
With the past, the same as me

It would be easier on Father's Day
If you were not here as a memory
I'm sure when you are gone from us
We'll celebrate your anniversary

As it is for now we'll deal with it
In the best way in which we can
And that for me is not to hate you
Instead, try for us to be friends

I give you this card from a store
A message that I cannot write
Hoping that this simple jester
Will try to make matters right

It says that I love you always
And will always be there for you
This is a Father's Day card
Saying the words I can't do

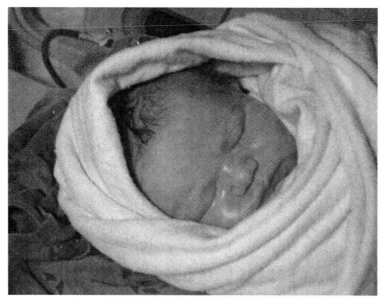

Father's Day Gift

There is no finer gift to give
Than the one of new life
My gift on Father's Day
A present from my wife

There she was a tiny girl
Premature by a week or two
Now that I am a new father
What on earth do fathers do

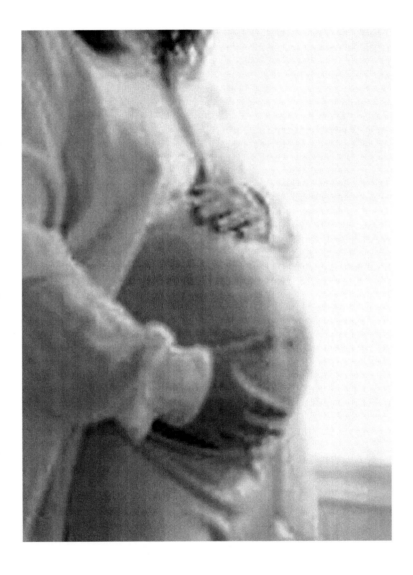

Tiny Pill

I've take, take, taken
My pill

Now I should have
Taken another
Then I wouldn't have
Become a mother

Oh just that one
Little tiny pill
I wouldn't have got
Pregnant from Bill

I was so young
And very naive
His lying stories
I did believe

He said that he
Loved me as no other
Now I'm going to
Become a mother

This my warning
Of advice
Marry him first
Become his wife

Get those marriage
Vows said
Before you spend
That time in bed

If it's a mother
You want to be
You'll be married
To raise your baby

Leslie Stewart: Go'Way!

It's better to
Have that gold ring
Or then this song
You might sing

I've take, take, taken
My pill

Now I should have
Taken another
Then I wouldn't have
Become a mother

Working hard

Work is not all it's made up to be
Work is not the life, meant for me
I'm a lazy guy, and proud to say
I'll leave that work for another day

I don't have to do, all that work to-day
I can put it off, for another day
Too much work, I have to say
I'm very lazy, I like it this way

Too much work for one guy
It's all piled up to the sky
I'm beat before I even begin
There's no way in hell that I can win

I lay in bed, dreaming of work to do
If I had a buddy, he would do it for you
When I was just a little skinny kid?
I had a friend, all the work he did.

Lost my friend in a pile of go-an-do-its
Couldn't find him, when I looked through it
He was the only friend I ever had
The thought of it now, makes me sad

I don't know why there's so much for one guy
If I only had a little work, sure I would try
If I could only put a handle on it, one time
Start early in the morning, that would be fine

I'm not afraid of work, its just not fun
They say hard work never killed anyone
My back is sore, and my knees ache
Fingers are numb—stop me now for goodness sake

I can feel time starting to slip away
Maybe I'll leave it all for another day
I know my doctor, that's what she would do
Tell me to stay away, work is not for you

Maybe some day I'll give it an honest try
I know there's hope for me, I'm not a stupid guy
My psychologist said, "It was well beyond my scope
But I should never really, give up hope"

The weather man seems a job I could try
Call for snow, rain, wind, clouds or blue sky.
I'm full of hot air and have wind at my back
I could do that job it seems some slack

I could try calling the races at the C.D.P.C.
That might be the job best suited for me
They don't go anywhere, just run around twice
I like the name, *Somebeachsomewhere,* sounds nice

My wife was reading the paper, give this a try
I looked her way and she had a sparkle in her eye
Called for a man, low in drive and self a steam
But I'm no politician and boy was that mean.

All this talk of working is getting me down
I better go find a couch, and not make a sound
My eyes are getting tried, soon I'll be asleep
My kind of shepherd has only one sheep

So take this advice from a lazy man
Just do as little work, if you can
Let your wife do, all she can do
Just tell her, "Honey I love you."

A Place To Sat

There was no place to be sat
Because the hair off our black cat
Covered the couch and the chairs
With its discarded old cat hair

She would lazily look up at you
As if to say, "How do you do"
There's no point in sitting down
Not a clean spot to be found

The behind of our good pants and jeans
Looked like an old horror movie I'd seen
The return of the Island Wolf man
A forbidden creature of the land

No doubt he also had a shedding cat
Leaving grey and black hair where he sat
I vacuumed the hair off the couch the other day
It was covered in no time the same old way

That old cat was up sprawled about
Get off there, I gave her a shout
She just looked at me in a pathetic way
Was there something I wanted to say?

My wife thought if we had two-sided tape
We could wear it on our bums when we ate
The hair would stick to the tape—not our jeans
We were the hairiest-ass family you ever seen

Let's solve the problem, get clear of the cat
Then there would be no problem where we sat
Now that idea had a very short life span
She could live with the cat, get clear of the man

The gift

Not that smart
Not that bright,
Going like hell
On a wet
Stormy night

Just a light
In the rear view
Mirror,
He passed us
As if we
Weren't here

We were just
Putt-in along,
Wipers singing
That old
Swoosh, swoosh
Swoosh song

As they went
Sailing on by,
Stirred up snow
We couldn't see
Thought that was
A stupid guy

Took my foot
Off the gas,
He had no
Taillights
Man this guy
Is an ass
He was gone

Driving fast,
Disappeared into
The stormy night
It scared us
To be passed

My heart slowed
Down to a beat,
It was racing
Suddenly I had no
Feeling in
My feet

We slipped left
We slipped right,
I didn't see
That car
On the road
Tonight

It had bounced
Off a tree,
Into a ditch
Over a hill
Across the road
Smashed into me

We spun around
Air bags blew,
A blast of cold
Winter air
The windshield
Was gone I knew

The gift

Our seatbelts worked
Holding us tight,
What kind of
An idiot
Tried to kill
Us tonight

We sat in silence
Of smashing sounds,
Another car
Crashed into us
Spinning our
Car around

We became
Well aware,
Our lives
Were in danger
Time to get away
Can't sit here

We limped away
Into the night,
Lying on a
Snow bank
Ever so scared
Out of our life

All the crashing
It was done,
Three cars
On the road
Tangled together
Making one

Someone screamed
Then another,
A child
No it's two
Help, help
Save our mother

The other car
Not a sound,
Just a hissing
Motor running
Sparks flying
No one around

We could hear
Sirens far away,
Coming to this
Bad accident
On Christmas day

We crawled down
From the bank,
As help
Did arrive
We prayed
And gave thanks

The children's
Mother was OK,
The firemen
Cut away the
Wreckage and
Save them today

The gift

The third car
No one around,
They looked
Inside, outside
But no bodies
They found

The windshield
Was missing too,
Broken door glass
It looks now
As if both bodies
Went through

Not in the
Wrecked car,
The policemen
Started to
Looked around
Not that far

Up in a tree
An awful sight,
A teenaged person
Looks like
A girl
Dressed in white

The other body
Was soon found,
A young man
Was dead
Neck broken
On the ground

The five survivors
Hospital bound,
Very much
Glad to be
Alive tonight
Not as a body found

Innocent people
Driving home,
On this stormy
Christmas night
A speeding driver
Talking on a phone

The last words
That he said,
To his mother
Were "I'll be
Home soon"
Now he's dead

His sister is
Gone too,
Their mother's
Only children
Died in a crash
Involving you

It's a sad gift
This Christmas day,
Five will live
Bearing scars
Two others died
A horrible way.

A Friend's Journey

Going to bury
A good friend today
He'll take a journey
To a place far away

We have sad eyes
And grieving hearts
We'll wish him well
When he departs

Childhood memories
Of a good friend
Inseparable buddies
When older men

We watched our children
As they all grew
Our boys we said
"Look like me and you"

We sang our last
Burial Hymn
Deep down inside
I'm going with him

I hold the hands
Of my family tight
Knowing I won't
Sleep for many a night

I'll miss my special
Childhood friend
Knowing that someday
We'll be together again

Married on a Holiday

Ola came to the island
From so far away
Her intention was
Just a brief holiday

Taking the ferry ride
She saw the red shore
This was her first time
She had never been before

A small cabin at High Bank
Just a short week to rent
Halfway through the week
This letter home she sent

I have fallen in love
With red rocks and sand
I will marry this paradise
Of Prince Edward Island

Sweet is the fragrant
Sea brisk air, fields of green
Wild flowers and peaceful times
No other place have I seen

I write this my letter
On the shore of red clay
How a woman fell in love
On a summer holiday

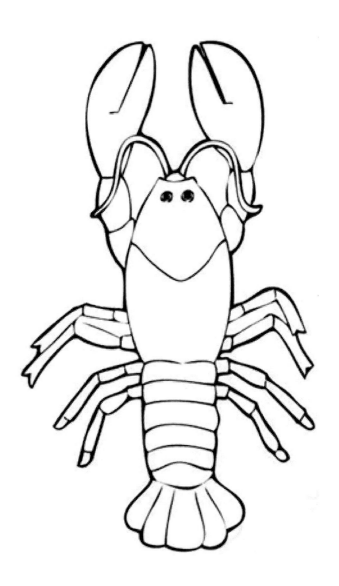

Starving Kitten

Poor little starving kitten
Why do you look like that?
Can't you find field mice
Or a big fat juicy rat

You need to go hunting
Put some meat on those bones
Get out in the farmer's field
And make yourself at home

Eat like your forefather
The king of the jungle Lions
Not sitting on my back porch
Meowing loud and crying

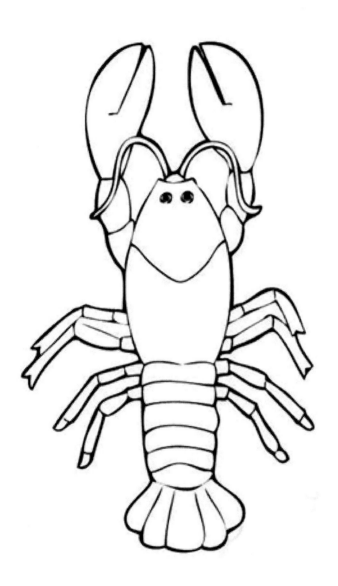

Small Shoppers

Little kids shopping
Down at the mall
In this big world
They seem so small

Holding mommy's hand
Shopping in stores
Looking up at things
Small necks are sore

Much closer to gum
Stuck on the floor
Than in machines
Outside of the stores

Just bend down low
And pick up the gum
Here Mom, do you
Want to have some?

Little sweaty hands
Just want to feel
Come on Mom
What's the big deal?

Now don't touch
Moms do say
I don't have the
Money for it today

Political Flowers

Political flowers
Are easy to grow
Plant them deep
Protect from snow

Plant a red bulb
A blue one or green
You can get orange
Bulbs now it seems

Plenty of fresh water
Fertilize every day
Watch them grow into
A political display

They'll be popping up
Out of the ground
Making a beautiful
Garden, I've found

Liberal bright red
Conservative deep blue
NDP brilliant orange
And the Green Party too

As political flowers
Grow into a display
It's all that fertilizer
They bloom this way

Magnificent red flower
Gorgeous dark blue
Orange petals glowing
Green stems and leaves too

I watch my flowers
Move to and fro
With all that fertilizer
Things sure can grow

They move in the wind
Sway from left to right
Very seldom are straight
As most politicians might

They give off a scent
A fragrant flower
Each trying to beat
The one with the power

It's the stem and leaf
Green, holds them up
Keeping the blossoms
From being corrupt

If they work together
Orange, blue and red
Green will hold them up
Organic fertilizer fed

I love all of my
Political flowers
And as the gardener
I have the power

It's I who waters
It's I who feeds
It's I who prunes
It's you needs me

Trains are gone

We're going back, back
To the golden days
When trains left their
Tracks on island clay

From Wood Islands
To Tignish to Souris
Iona to Charlottetown
People were in a hurry

The new modern days
Had arrived on PEI
You could take a trip
Go for a train ride

The old horse and buggy
Bicycle or travel by feet
None of that now, my boy
Take the train, have a seat

You could now move all
Your produce of Wheat
Potatoes, Corn and Cabbage
The train you couldn't beat

It was faster then most
Transportation at the time
Sturgeon to Charlottetown
And back for just a dime

The town of Montague
Had the roundabout
"Spin the table top"
The engineer did shout

Down at the harbour
Was the end of the line
Checking your watch
She was always on time

The whistle would blow
Hot steam began to spew
As little kids we ran
The steam did burn you

It hissed from its nostrils
Roared, clanged and clatter
Spinning its wheels around
My teeth began to chatter

The trembling of the earth
Moved beneath my feet
The monster was leaving
The memory of this I keep

Away it went roaring
Leaving its own tracks
Every station the same
The trains will come back

I grew up in no time
With changes all around
We build better roads
Now: no trains to be found

Even the tracks are gone
No traces left in the clay
There are only the beds where
Trains travelled each day

Take your bikes and ride
The Confederation Trail
You can still hear the sounds
Taste the coal burning smell

Root Cellar

We went over to our good neighbours
The other day to see their new deck
Well it's their only patio deck ever
So we all went over to check

We all cosied up in some patio chairs
Commenting on how lovely it was becoming
Now the old guy was doing some finishing
Adding some vertical pieces while humming

If he had played a fiddle tune or two
I'm sure I could've danced up a storm
As it was he didn't, but joined the conversation
After all it was Canada Day, the weather warm

Topics of this and that and what's goin' on?
"Nice to not have the woodstove burning," I say
"Yes," he did say, "But all that hot weather
Was some hot for us on Canada Day."

I had always wanted to ask that question
Where was his firewood piled anyways?
We have known them some five years or so
And had never seen firewood to this day

So no more holding back, I'll just ask
"Have you got firewood for next season"?
"Not all of it but fairly soon we will"
"Why do you ask"? "Oh for no reason"

"Well," said I, "There is this curiosity"
"I can smell it. I see the smoke from the flue
I know you burn wood to heat with in winter
The door is sometimes open when we visit you"

"Your house is always so hot and cosy
So we know you burn lots of firewood
But, but we never see cords of it
No wood chips, no mess, like there should"

"We buy our firewood from your son
He delivers four to five cords in the fall"
"But when we visit or look over here
You have no piles of firewood at all"

Now I felt proud I was doing all right
So many questions, he had to answer one
There was a long silence and then he spoke
"You buy your firewood from my son?"

This was not the answer I was looking for
He had won again, I sat silent in my chair
"Do you see that tall Willow tree here?
And the Oak and the Maple tree over there?"

Well he had planted them all
Over some fifty long years ago
About ten years after that in late spring
He had gone down to the cellar, like so

Just a small pile of wood left to burn
He noticed something sticking in the wall
It was the root of a tree, had lost its way
He gave it no mind until early that fall

We had cut the firewood just as you say
All blocked, split, ready to be stored below
In the cellar, kept dry for the coming winter
Well, a surprise to us all just to let you know

From those three trees the roots did grow
Through the cellar walls, over the floors
We had to cut up all those tree roots
So now, firewood we gather up no more

Some forty years of not going into the woods
Cutting down trees to burn as firewood
We just go down into our root cellar
For our home is root heated, firewood

Backhoe Joe (two)

I've heard those rumors about this guy
Digs a trench deep, digs them deep and wide
Digs a footing for a town or two
They're quite happy and say that will do

He dug this trench over Alberton way
He did the whole thing in just a day
Dug from the ocean to make Casumpec Bay
Now they have a harbour and like it that way

A lady from O'Leary, she had some cows
Needed a trench dug but didn't know how
She had to get water to her herd to drink
He dug her, a trench from Carleton, I think

They say it must be a very old rig, doing OK
How old is it? No one can really say
Some say he got it after the Great War
Others say he had it long a long time before

I've heard stories about Malpeque Bay
It used to be a big hill back in its day
They needed sand dunes over Cavendish way
That kept backhoe Joe busy for many a day

So backhoe Joe what do you say
Are you out there digging a trench today?
I heard you quit drinking while working away
The Hillsborough trench is now a water way

There was this big storm off Boughton Bay
With his backhoe, Joe he saved the day
Annandale was about to be swept out to sea
He made that spit of land, keeping them safe as can be

If you're ever over Cardigan point you know
Remember, backhoe Joe he dug it just so
They said "they needed three rivers and a bay"
He filled in Panmure causeway to make it this way

Folks from Murray River and the Harbour they know
That backhoe Joe, he was a heading their way slow
Joe was to widen the river from the bridge to the bay
By morning Murray Harbours north and south you say

The last time I heard tell of backhoe Joe
He was making the ski hill at Brookvale grow
He was taking the mud from Victoria by the sea
They hope to have a harbour for the island's navy

No other man has done so much in his time
As backhoe Joe did to P.E.I. and it looks fine
He made her more, shapely out of the red clay
God couldn't have done better Himself they say

Backhoe Joe, does anybody know this backhoe Joe?

Island driving

If you're here from away
Better heed what I say
This is why islanders
Drive this way

Watch how we drive
Our patience is as short
As the island is wide
We drive like bees from a hive

Stop signs are for you,
We just drive right through
No point in stopping
We got way too much to do

Got to get that coffee
We need a our fix
We drink it black
No cream or sugar to mix

Still a mystery to me
Those lines on the road
Double lines, single lines
Some dotted all in a row

Some guy had paint and
Nothing better to do
He drove around the island
Confusing me and you

We got some weird signs
Stop, turn right
My wife and I sat there
The whole darn night

We wanted to turn left
Go Wood Islands way
So just turn left
The sign had to say

There's no better driver
Then us in bad weather
With studded tires,
Slow now? Hell, not ever

These aren't ordinary roads
This is our raceway.
We drive her hard and fast
All night and all day

Fast straight away
And hair tight bends
We fly over ladder hill
Land back down again

If our style of driving
Isn't suited for you
Close one eye, foot to the floor
And that will have to do,

Potato trucks, in the fall
Cover our roads with spuds
Those don't bother us at all
Hell, they must be duds.

I saw a fellow from away
On the road pick-en up fallen spuds.
As I drove by, heard him say
Which one of you is bud?

Move over coming through
Got me a two horse trailer
And you better stay back
Nothing worst, then flying poo

Once they hit a little car
Covered hood and glass
He had come here from afar
Last thing he saw was a horse's ass

Shopping at Home

I was sent once again shopping
To the Home Hardware Store
My wife has sent me there
Many, many times before

Go buy some wallpaper
And don't forget the paste?
Oh pick up another roll
In case you make a mistake

Buy a gallon of house paint
A nice shade of pink will do
I need some more light bulbs
Oh better buy a dozen or two

If you see Darryl or Donald
Ask about the kitchen sink
Don't forget a new deodorizer
The bathroom is starting to stink

They had a deal in the flyer
Buy something get another free
It might be in the garden section
Get one for you, the other for me

The toaster is on the blink
It only toasts the one side
I like my whole bread toasted
A two slice or four I can't decide

They have some wind chimes
Get a nice metal one for me
No, pick-up two of them for us
I want the neighbours to see

Leslie Stewart: Go 'Way!

Better get some Canadian flags
And get an island one as well
We'll fly them all so proudly
We're patriotic, people can tell

Now here is some money
Don't go spending it all
We still have to go shopping
At the Down East Mall.

Click-it-de-clack

Train, train
What do you say?
Riding the rails
Over our red clay

Part of our history
Helped us to grow
As you steamed along
In summer and snow

From tip to tip
From side to side
We travelled together
On your train ride

You carried our hopes
You carried our dreams
We heard your whistle
Blowing off steam

My grandfather said
"The trains chugged along
Over the countryside
Singing their songs"

As the giant steel wheels
Came down on the track
Making its musical sound
Click, click-it-de-clack

The engineer yelled
Out from the train
We're leaving now
We'll be back again

Train, train
You went away
Never to return
To our red clay

Dancing with the Stove

I swear that's what my mother did
She spent most of her life, dancing with the stove
Doing our breakfast of porridge and bacon and eggs
Making lunch, dinner, always doing bread loaves

In early morning to the last thing at night
Mom danced with pots and pans and firewood
Boiling the kettle for their coffee or tea
Stoking the kitchen stove the best she could

Piles of split kindling lying beside the stove
The old hound slept under the stove at night
Oil cloth flooring with sheet metal on top
Sat the kitchen stove, the center piece all right

Old black pipe rose out from the top of the stove
Reaching up to the ceiling, through that floor
Into the room above, then passing into the attic
Out the roof, were sparks flew ever more

When it was laundry day summer or winter
Large monstrous pots sat on the stove to boil
Mom had a washing machine, with wringers
In summer it was hot work, what toil

The winter I guess was better for doing the wash
Mom had the fire going to heat our old home
She heated the water to wash the clothes, to hang
They froze hard as boards, hanging outside alone

We would bring them back into the house and stack
Pants and shirts stretched out frozen hard as can be
Piled in the kitchen to be thawed by the stove heat
My mom, "Don't break an arm or leg," said she

The eating table was in the kitchen as well
Many chairs placed around that eating board
On one wall under the window, our kitchen sink
By another wall a chair, my father sat, often snored

Difficult to remember, for I was very young
My older brothers and sisters, we're nine in all
We had a large family, for such a small house
A living room, then upstairs three bedrooms small

The bathroom used to be outside before my time
Now we have a toilet, sink and a claw foot tub
On that kitchen stove water boiled for our bath
We carried the water upstairs to have a scrub

Like the old dog, I would lay under the stove
The best place to hide on cold and stormy days
Mom was always dancing around the kitchen
Under the stove I saw shoes and socks at play

Brothers and sisters some doing their homework
Sitting at the table, mom helped with what she could
But too many children, would always cause a fight
Sometimes they got theirs, by a piece of firewood

The radio played my mother's favourite songs
It sat on the window sill, clothes hanger for antenna
The off white plastic, close to a smoke yellow color
Or maybe when new, it was the color of a banana

No matter the color, it gave my mother some joy
Now as I think of it, between that yellow radio
And that old kitchen wood stove we had
This would sum up most of her life that I know

I think some of the best days for our mother
When the children were at work or school
My older brothers and sisters had to work
The rest of us tried to learn not to be fools

Mom would be at home baking for supper
Talking to the stove and listening to the radio
This must have been her quiet time alone
A special time for her to heal the soul

Mom and Dad had ten children in all
The oldest died when she was very young
Nine grew up as she danced with the stove
I wonder what her favourite song was, she sung.

Most of us grow up and then leave the family home
Mom dancing with the wood stove, will always remain
The everlasting picture of that large family of nine
When my older brothers and sisters left, it wasn't the same

Time had treated her hard dancing all those years
Her feet had swollen, her legs got tired too fast
Too many dances with the laundry, baking, cooking
These are my memories, of that time past

No Ordinary Sunday

It's Sunday morning and I'm sitting in church, listening to the sermon, but not taking much in unfortunately. My mind is on a sore ankle that was now holding me up as we sang a song of joy. There is no joy in a swollen ankle caused by a blocked shot in last night's hockey loss. We had played our usual hockey game of give and take; however the other team gave more hits and took more shots, giving us one goal and taking five goals for themselves. My mind was going over that game and how poorly I had played at times, plus what I was going to do after church today.

We had no game today; and it was unusual to not be playing hockey on a Sunday. There are only a few Sundays off that we have in a long hockey season and with the playoff just around the corner, it was nice to get that break. February is upon us, giving us our fourth month of cold, blasting winter. It had started to snow back in November. At first it would snow, then melt, then snow some more, then take longer to melt. Just before Christmas the snow no longer melted.

For those who wanted a white Christmas, their wish came true and I wished them well for that. Now maybe my wish will come true for an early spring, green grass, warm sun, hockey is over, no more cuts and swollen ankles, we win the championship and all is well on the island.

Church is letting out; I'll head for home and have some lunch, maybe grilled cheese and some hot tomato soup. I see some of the players from my team that attend this church, others go to different churches and some, well, don't attend church at all. I say, "Hi" to my coach and his lovely daughter Mary Beth St Clair. My thoughts remain on his daughter, forgetting to say anything to her mother. Her father had said many times I did suffer from some kind of memory loss problem which may have lead to my inability to play better hockey.

Last night's performance hadn't impressed Mary Beth very much and it felt colder now than it had earlier in the morning, leaving me to my thoughts of grilled cheese and hot tomato soup. So much for that grilled cheese and soup: my mother had forgotten to get sliced cheese and I didn't like that white cheese my father ate.

The tomato soup went well with toasted white bread and peanut butter and sliced banana. Nothing better than hot peanut butter melting, running down your face and clinging to the bottom of your chin—this is a Sunday lunch.

"Leslie, can you shovel the sidewalk after you have eaten?" asked my Mom. I sit glancing across the room at my two older brothers, but their names are not mentioned in this cleaning of the sidewalk. Then again my footprints were the only ones coming and going to the house this morning. This was my mother's reason for asking me as it seems I have the only pair of winter boots, which I never wore to church. The boots are a size eleven and no doubt bigger than the feet of my two brothers, who not only have small brains but smaller feet sizes too, making it impossible for them to ever fill the shoes of their younger brother.

"Sure mom, I'll do that for you, and maybe shovel the road as well. Wouldn't want anybody to get snow on their delicate little running shoes," I replied. For that smart remark I received a sharp backhander to my head from dear mother.

I have two close friends and both play hockey with me, Lloyd and Larry. Lloyd and I play defence together. He wears number two and I wear number three. My other friend Larry is one of our top goal scorers and could some day make it to the pros, we think. As for Lloyd and I, our future in hockey is house league at its best. It's not the fame we seek as great players; we like our friends and enjoy the game. It gives us a chance to travel to different towns and play hockey.

It is a chance to intermix with hockey moms and dads from other communities in the area. A chance to play hockey in other arenas, hit their sons, slamming them into the boards or body checking them at centre ice, and even scoring some goals from time to time. They call us names and throw water or spit at us and if we win, they often throw eggs or worse things at our bus. Winter and hockey is indeed the best environment for growing boys to become men or at least adults.

But this Sunday, we have a day we shall never forget.

Around one o'clock we start to gather on the town street corner, some have been there a short time. Others like Larry and I have come together to meet our buddies on a cold but sunny Sunday afternoon.

It was the usual talk for boys that we came upon; talk about our poor play last night. Then out of nowhere Bill says he had his best game of the season so far. Strange now, as no one disagreed with him on that. You see, Bill has to be our worst player of all time, so any improvement would be noticed by him the most. We agree with our hockey buddy that he did have a stellar game last night and we're now expecting better things of him in games to come, and our play off hopes rest on his bony shoulders.

In a short time we had become a small circle of teenagers, some one year older, others one year younger. Larry and I were the same age, born in the same month of September, in fact. The group talked about what to do and not to do, which did bring some laughter and causing some burping and with that farting, as it seems one goes with the other.

Now talk about a head shaker and holy shit, Lloyd had our attention real quick. He was walking towards us at his usual shovelling pace, the smell of Old Dutch Pipe Tobacco filled the cold fresh air, air we had so easily taken for granted, causing some of the boys to move back from the crowded circle.

Mike and Ronnie were both saying at the same time if they got smoke on their clothes they'd get shit from their parents, and they moved away from Lloyd in a hurry. I'd never seen them move that quick, so fast in fact that Bill stepped on Ronnie's foot causing some pain and some choice words to follow.

"So guys, what's going on?" asks the Lloyd. I still couldn't believe he was standing there with that damned hooked pipe in his mouth. The pipe just off to the left side of his mouth, the smoke drifting up his cheek then into his into his left eye causing him to squint with it. No doubt the smoke had its effect on old Lloyd's eyesight.

He did make a good point though, in spite of the fact he was breaking the law and standing on a corner in the middle of town, just a half block from the police station.

No one seemed to have that, "Oh this is a hell-of-an-idea". Each of us just hoped the other guy would come up with that something-to-do idea. The chatter continued for some time with nothing coming of any of it. We could do that or this, we could play road hockey was another bright idea that went away faster than it came. No one had the answer.

It was now around two o'clock, Lloyd had long put his pipe away, making it easier to breathe again and less likely to get us into trouble with the law and our parents, smelling of smoke.

Some of the girls from town had now stopped by to ask, "What's going on?" and our usual reply was, "Not much." There was Mary Beth St'Clair, with her know-it-all girlfriends, all dressed up for a winters walk.

Now Mary Beth was wearing a large fur hat and wearing a long white nylon jacket, beautiful white and blue mittens and a blue dress. On her feet were mukluks, but those legs of hers seemed to have no protection at all? Well boys can be boys and I was a boy, remembering her sharp tongue and cold shoulder from earlier today at church. I picked up a handful of snow and ever so gently tossed it on her bare legs and down into her white Mukluks.

"We now have something to do boys: run for your lives!" Those were my words as Lloyd, Larry and I ran down the street, away from trouble.

In the receding distance we could hear Mary Beth calling, "Wait until my father gets you, Leslie Stewart!" I just wanted to savour that moment, remembering the look of shock on her face. She was right about one thing, her dad will no doubt have his way with us at practice on Tuesday, but it's not Tuesday yet.

We ran down the main street of our small town for only a couple of short blocks and came upon the end of the road, as you might say. You see, on the island most main streets run towards water of some kind. It might be a river or a bay, and in our case we find ourselves face to face with the ocean.

Remembering that it is February and not the middle of summer, we have no beach of red sand to make our escape along. No, we have ice.

No one is chasing us anyway so no need to run any further, but the ice is inviting for us boys and with out much prompting form each other away we went.

My father had said to me once that, in years gone by when he was a kid, the towns people used to have ice boats and sail for miles over the large fields of ice. Today the water never settles down and freezes fast enough to form those amazing sheets of ice; all we get now are tall piles of ice pushed against each other, grinding with the wind making eerie sounds, mostly at night.

There are some small flat sheets of ice we run and slide on, avoiding the cracks so as not to trip over them or into them. Ice is very hard, no matter where you fall.

The sun is warm on our faces but there is a sharp chill in the air as we walk along over the ice, not going anywhere in particular except further away from shore.

Lloyd remembers he has his pipe and lots of tobacco and taking them out of his pockets, begins lighting up. I have my own pipe hidden in the lining of my long coat and bravely take it out, asking, "Can I have some of that Old Dutch?" We are good buddies and think a lot alike. Not to be outdone, Larry also has a small pipe in his pocket along with a different smell of fragrant pipe tobacco, but Old Dutch just the same.

We continue our walk over the ice field, slowly but surely heading out to the open sea away from the safety of shore.

Along our way we have clambered over many high piles of ice that been formed by the sea pushing against the sea ice causing it to ride high in the air. In that process making some beautiful sculptured shapes, with deep blues and light blue ice you can see through and in others you can get a reflection of your self smoking your pipe with your two best friends.

At times we hear the creaking of the ice, as it shifts from the sea waves still rolling well beneath it. The ice is no doubt plenty thick as it's been fastened to the shore for a month or more.

Lots of times we have walked on the ice pack, along with most of the people from town. Some families come out to play hockey or the girls figure skate on the small flat surfaces that have formed because of the sea flooding up through a crack.

We, however, have never been this far out from shore that I can remember, as I turn my head to look back at the distant houses and docks.

Suddenly Lloyd stops and points to a dark shape as it moves slowly along the ice: a seal. As we look at the seal another one climbs out of the water, no doubt through an air hole in the ice. We carefully watch, making no sudden moves. Now within a few moments as many as six seals have come out of the water, taking what looks like a sun bath.

The wind is now blowing a little stronger off shore and the seals get there first whiff of Old Dutch Pipe Tobacco. They look about, not knowing what to look for; it just isn't a smell they are used to, and we're dressed in our heavy winter clothes, looking somewhat like seals, I think.

No panic from the seals at this point, just curiosity, and that is what Larry also must have felt as he jumped up and ran at the seals, his arms waving, smoke coming out his mouth, creating all kinds of havoc.

Larry ran towards the open water hole, as if to cut off the seals' retreat to safety. This was a dumb thing to do.

We watched from our safe distance, not wanting to be part of whatever Larry was going to do. Sometimes it is better to observe an idiot, than to be one.

Oh the seals moved faster than Larry could have imagined, off the ice and into that hole in no time flat. By the time Larry got to that hole in the ice, he was the only wildlife left huffin' and puffin'.

We calmly walked towards our idiot friend who was standing, looking down into the hole as if he had lost something. Lloyd asked, "What did you think would happen when you chased them, they would just sit there?"

We hadn't got to the hole as yet, but were close enough to see one of the larger seals come back out of that hole that Larry was looking down into.

The seal grabbed his boot then his leg and started to drag our buddy into the water. We got there in time for each of us to grab his coat and arms. Lloyd took a quick kick at the seals head, making contact, causing the seal to strike at Lloyd's foot, letting go of Larry's leg. A near miss but that's all we needed to get away from the hole in the ice and that pissed off seal. By now we were far enough from the hole, just as the seal came up again to survey for dinner options: it wouldn't be us.

We were, let's say, some upset with ourselves, and my heart was racing faster than in any hockey game I had ever played in. We had reached the end of the ice field as far as I was concerned. Smoking and being seal meal was way too much excitement on this Sunday.

With a hole in his boot from the seal's teeth, Larry felt damp but proud to share this experience with his best buddies.

I felt it was time to head for home and shore. Home was a long way away as we turned around and took notice as to just how far it was.

The sun that had been warm and inviting, was now cooling down as the wind picked up, blowing cold east air into our faces.

My pipe had been lost in the fight with the seal, and the other two had put theirs away as we headed for home, climbing over those ice castles that earlier had intrigued us, but now acted more as speed bumps slowing our retreat from the ice field.

The noise of the cracking of the ice beneath seemed to get worse as the sun went down and the wind picked up blowing harder in our faces. We were making some headway slowly toward the shore, and the lights of the houses became easier to make out.

Our hands and feet were freezing along with my nose, which couldn't take much cold as it turned out. We didn't talk much about the seals or the smoking; we concentrated more on our footing and the quickest way home in the dark, not wanting any more trouble.

Larry did remark that he felt like an Arctic explorer looking for the North Pole, or was it the South Pole? "Where did those men get lost and freeze to death?" he finished with.

**** It was seven o'clock when we arrived safely back on the island shore of frozen snow. As for the frozen sea ice we had just crossed, it was nice to see it over our shoulders.

We headed for our homes Larry and I went along together and Lloyd went his way, Larry had quite a limp by now the seal had not only bit into his boot but had twisted his ankle in the struggle.

I said, "Good night!" to Larry and hoped his foot wasn't too bad and, "Are you going to tell your parents?" "No I don't think so," he said.

"I might have to lose that boot with the holes in it, so as not to have dad find it and ask about the teeth marks".

I went into my house and said hello to mom and went up stairs to run a hot bath. "How was your day Leslie William?" said my mom. "Oh it was just another ordinary Sunday," I said.

The next morning after eating breakfast, I was out the door and zipping up my jacket will walking to the road, I turned to go down the street to catch the bus for school. From our driveway I could see the shore line that was only about half a dozen blocks away. But today I stopped in my tracks as my chin must have dropped to the ground. There before my eyes I could see open water at the shore, where only yesterday we had walked out over two miles of frozen ice.

In the far distance I could see just the fine edge of the ice field, the ice field that we had been walking on the day before, it must have been moving as we headed for home last night.

My stomach felt very sick as I walked down that road and waited for the bus.

Other school kids waited there talking about things they had done yesterday or watched on T.V. last night.

Larry joined us with his brother's winter boots on. He said that he had mislaid his and did I see the ice was all gone? "Oh yes," I said.

Nothing more was said until the school bus came and we got on. There sitting at the back of the bus as we always did was Lloyd. "Did you see the ice has moved from the shore?" he said. "It's a good thing no one was out there when it moved last night, how would any one know they where even on it and how could you look for them if they were?" he said.

"Yes aren't we the lucky ones for that, we stayed on shore yesterday and what did we do?" said I

Juniper

I remember sitting over at my neighbours
Bernard mentioned the word Juniper
We were discussing me doing some building
And I would be using a lot of 2x4s

I was going to build a back porch or veranda
Depending on how you us the term
Bernard said, "The best wood for outside
Was Juniper, it had strength and was firm"

This no doubt left me in very deep thought
We had just moved here from Ontario.
We had plenty of Junipers plants
Around the house, two types I know

The first type was a skyrocket Juniper
Some may reach 10 feet tall, 4in thick.
Ours grew up along side the house
Hiding the walls made of brick

The other style of Juniper
Was a spreading or sprawling type
Again found around lots of homes
Used under windows, they looked alright

I personally found these to be smelly
As if some cat had sprayed on them
As children we often played hide and seek
The Juniper was a good hiding place within

Again Junipers they did grow in the wild
Some were quite wide, coving the ground.
They were itchy to the skin, I will say
You were careful wearing shorts I found

Once when I was horseback riding through the woods
We came upon a bush that was hiding a rabbit
The horse veered sharply to the left when surprised
I went sliding through the juniper bush, damn it

I remember this all to well as you can tell
But am ever so grateful the branches were small
If this was the tree that 2x6 came from
Believe me I wouldn't be here now at all

So what is a Juniper? What do they look like?
I asked my friend and neighbour Bernard for advice
He said, "Everyone knows what a Juniper looks like."
How come a smart guy like me didn't know this, right?

His description was lacking in some detail
The tree was tall, thick and lots of them around
I knew a lot about trees, I had worked in the bush
Most trees looked much like this, I had found

I was going to Murray River with Bernard
To get a truck load of shaving for horse bedding
As we drove along Point Pleasant rd, to the river
To see Jerry at the saw mill, we were heading

Just what does this Juniper tree look like?
As we drove along, the bush and water passed us
Bernard said when he found some trees
He would let me know. "Stop making such a fuss."

"There's some now, look over there see them?"
Well I did look and I did see some trees
But now this is the big but, do they have
Any of those things we called leaves?

As all of these were covered in needles
Most of them were yellow or gone
Yes, yes those are the Juniper trees
What I saw for a tree was all wrong

These were not Juniper tress as I know
These were Larch or Tamarack trees
A very, hard softwood that has needles
They lose some of them like leaves

As other softwoods stay green all year
These trees have their needles turn yellow
Bernard had never heard those names
This only confirmed I was a strange fellow

We let the names of trees stay as they were
As we both have been known to fib a bit
He knew he was right and I knew I was right
But, that was not going to be the end of it

That winter well attending night school
A man from the lands and forest of P.E.I
Came to our class telling us about the forest
He seemed to be a smart enough guy

So I asked the question what is a Juniper
He said "On the island or off the island"
"Oh, on," said I. The Juniper is really a Larch
Or Tamarack, we call it a Juniper on the island

Rusty M, Nails

Now this is a true story, well
About this old fellow named Nails
Others say it's a rumor you know
He was a moon shiner the story goes

Over the years he learned how
He's one of the best brewers now
It took a long time to get it right
And not getting caught as you might

People would talk about where to get some brew
Folks from North Cape, Souris and Little Pond knew
As folks talked, the Mounties were listening
Nails was doing more, than fishing and whistling

Folks around North Cape, Souris and Little Pond
Thought Nails and the law, they must got on
Because when the law came, Nails he knew
The Mounties never did find his homemade brew

Now in order to become a successful business man
And our moon shiner, Nails had a dandy plan
Not only did he talk to folks, he would preach
We should always have some goal in life, to reach

"Don't be drinking alcohol, it's the devils way
If you start, the devil will be at your door someday,"
Nails often told folks that, when a Mountie was in sight
He really meant, "Fresh brew was ready for tonight."

He had another way of throwing the law off his trail
When you went into his house, only old varnish you'll smell
Nails, is a coffin or casket maker, sort of a side line
He always had a brush or two dipped in bad turpentine

It seems when the law would pay a visit by surprise
You see, Nails lived outside of town just on a rise
He had the only house on the lane, no others were near
They only found Nails adding another coat of clear

You could look out the shed window and see the town
You could also see the Mounties, if they were around
This was a good location for the final touches of the brew
Now most recipients of the brew, never let on they knew

Our boy Mister Nails, never sold a casket or coffin
You see he revarnished that same one, quite often
The stench of the old varnish, covered the smell
The basement was full of shine, but you couldn't tell

So remember what I said, "True story or not"
In a well varnished casket, that will never rot
Sleeps Rusty M. Nails who is buried, well below
Folks from Souris, North Cape and Little Pond know

So now we have it, a moral of a sad story
When you start drinking you better worry
And it's one we hear most often
Are you adding another nail to a coffin?

GASPEREAUX

THERE ONCE WAS A MAN FROM GASPEREAUX,
WHO HAD A DOG AND TOGETHER THEY WOULD GO.

OFF TO SEA FOR LOBSTER AND FISH,
THAT FAITHFUL DOG, HE ATE FROM HIS DISH.
INTO THE BUSH THEY WOULD GO,
FOR FIREWOOD AND LUMBER
THAT DOG HE PULLED THOSE HEAVY LOGS
AND YET HE NEVER SLUMPERED

OH HOW THAT DOG DID SWEAR
THE MAN FROM GASPEREAUX AND HIS DOG DID GO.

MANY A TIME TO TOWN, THEY WOULD GO,
MASTER IN THE CAB WITH AIR, HEAT AND RADIO.
THE DOG IN THE BACK WALKING AROUND,
BUGS IN HIS TEETH, DIRT ON HIS FROWN
THE DOG HAD HEAT, ON HOT SUMMER DAYS
DIDN'T HAVE A HAT TOO KEEP OFF THE RAYS

OH HOW THAT DOG DID SWEAR,
THE MAN FROM GASPEREAUX AND HIS DOG DID GO.

THE DOG HAD AIR ON COLD WINTERY DAYS
EYES WATERING, THROAT SORE, HE HAD AIR.,
NO SCARF, NO TOUQUE, NO MITTENS TO WEAR.
MASTER IN THE CAB WITH HEAT, RADIO TO PLAY
PEOPLE WOULD LOOK AND PEOPLE WOULD SAY
HE LOVES HIS DOG, HIS DOG LOVE IT THAT WAY

OH HOW THAT DOG DID SWEAR
THE MAN FROM GASPEREAUX AND HIS DOG DID GO

WHEN TIME COMES AND IT DID ONE DAY,
THE MASTER, HE PASSED AWAY.
THE DOG VISITS HIS MASTER IN THE GROUND,
AS HE SITS NEAR BY, WITH THAT DOG LIKE FROWN.
REMEMBERING HIS TRIPS TO TOWN

OH HOW THAT DOG DID SWEAR
THE MAN FROM GASPEREAUX AND HIS DOG DID GO.

Lament for a Woodstove

If we had a woodstove
With a front glass door
We could lie on a bear rug
Right here on the floor

You with a glass of liquer
Me with a glass of wine
My arms wrapped in yours
Your arms wrapped in mine

The same thing could happen
On those damp fall days
In the heat from the fire
I'll feel the same way

In winter as the snow is softly
Falling outside on the ground
In front of the woodstove
On a bear rug we'd be found

I can see us cuddling
A kiss, more romance
But without the woodstove
This dream has no chance

Let's not waste any more time
A woodstove we have to get
It will be the finest gift
We have given each other yet

Deadly Gold

The Caribbean waters
Turquoise and deep blue
Priceless coral reefs
Home of tropical fish too

In the most beautiful
Gulf of Mexico
BP Oil drilled
For more black gold

They'd build a rig
This floating hell
Drilled the deepest
Dirtiest oil well

When it exploded
Killing eleven men
Will they now stop?
Or do it all again

Drill the ocean floor
Siphon the oil beneath
Having total disregard for
Protecting the coral reef

Species of fish and mammals
Crabs to oyster shells
Their ecological home
Replaced by an oily hell

Destroying marine life
Millions of years old
There'll be only pictures
And marine stories told

Of once the beautiful
Home to islands green
Where visitors travelled
Now none to be seen

Blackened sandy beaches
Covered in dead debris
Massive sickening oil slick
A reminder for us to see

It's best not to disturb
The nature of our land
The end of all nature
And the end of all man

Youth and Time

There was a time
When I knew what
I was thinking about
But I don't know
What time it is now

As a small boy walking
On Panmure Island Beach
Counting the endless waves
Dreaming of places afar
Smiling at my young life
That I had lived so far

In spring or late fall
The shores moved alone
No visitors' footsteps
Marked the virgin shore
Just those lapping waves
Some scouring sand crabs
A peace forever more

Time had no meaning
Just another perfect day
I alone roaming free
Having my adventures
Living my own dreams
Walking beside the sea

Watching fishing boats
Carve up the seas
Some going due east
Others west on this day
Do the fish below
Fish that I can't see
Do they swim this way?

Life was so easy
The next day was
Always same as the last
Morning, noon to night
The sun rose high
The moon shone bright

I always knew what
Was on my mind
Daydreaming mostly
Skipping a flat stone
Hiding in a dune
Just happy carefree
For being alone

The beach was my
Own sand timer
I didn't think of that
As each passing day
Of my own young life
The beach sands ran
Faster, faster away

Only a few grains of
Panmure Beach remain
Then, they're all gone
Life from a small boy
To an aging old man
Thinking of days past
My life on the island

To Pee or not to Pee

Oh I've got to stop and pee
Or it will burst inside of me

An old islander once told me,
"As a man you'll have to pee
You can always stop for a leak
Some of the girls will take a peek

"They will only take a short glance
When they see you drop your pants
You should use your zipper this way
It would be better if it was hid away."

A man can always stop for a pee
It's not the way that it should be
I don't know if it's wrong or right
Maybe they should only do it at night

I tell my children he's watering the plants
My daughter said, "It coming out his pants"
'Will it benefit all the flowers?" said she
As we past a group of men having a pee

I didn't know if it would or not
I wished they'd picked a better spot
Men can do it because they can
Stop for a leak on the Gentle Island

Maybe, just maybe pass a pee law
It's will be illegal to do what we saw
The question, "To pee or not to pee?"
On the side of the road like me

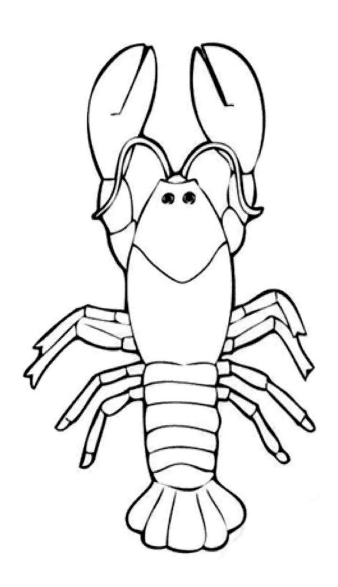

Spot

I've got a dog named Spot
And I like him a lot

We went down to the
Beach for a swim
Me and old Spot
He ran and jumped in
That's when I found out
Spot he couldn't swim
Sank to the bottom of the sea
Walked on the ocean floor
Back to play with me

I've got a dog named Spot
And I like him a lot

I got a brand new bike
But the bike, he didn't like
Spot chewed on a tire or two
But the rubber didn't pass through
He became constipated
Wished he hadn't ate it
I tied him up with the chain
And said never, never again

I've got a dog named Spot
And I like him a lot

Spot likes to chase cars
Once he ran so very far
We all thought that he was gone
Next morning, Spot on the lawn
Was chewing an Ontario Lic. Plate
Rest of the car he must have ate
We hope those nice folks from away
Will come back to visit another day

I've got a dog named Spot
And I like him a lot

My Golden Mirror

Two dastardly men
A refection of crime
Stole a Golden Mirror
That was mine

It had stood proudly
Up against the wall
Outside my Flower Shoppe
In the Down East Mall

On our Canada Day
Just after the hour of one
We saw this guy as he
Grabbed to make his run

Through the eyes
Of camera and lens
We watched the working
Of the two bad men

They studied their escape
And readied their plan
Then as one, not that bright
Of a dastardly man

Took my Golden Mirror
And made his getaway
Only to be arrested
In about twenty days

My Golden Mirror
Is back at the mall
Outside my Flower Shoppe
Fastened to the wall

To Wendy by Leslie

The Shoveller

There's a man with a shovel
And he's looking for snow
Cleaning sidewalks and driveways
Wherever he goes

From Montague to Brudenell
St. Peters to Georgetown
He cleans away all the snow
That's fallen on the ground

Dressed in Black or Blue,
Snow suits of Red or Pink
I did hear his name once
Now give me a minute to think

He sharpens his snow shovel
Well before early dawn
Then does his pre-shovelling
Exercise on his front lawn

I've seen him up east
In the small town of Souris
Snow was flying and melting
He was shovelling in a hurry

They say he's a snow thrower
Cleaning sidewalks and driveways
If you're driving around Kings County
For Heaven sakes get out of his way

Leslie Stewart: Go'Way!

Jetta Woman

I know this lady
From Sturgeon
And I know her
So very well
And this is her
Car story, I will tell

She didn't enjoy
Her silver, grey
KIA Spectra rig
She had no faith
As to how long
She could drive
Or how far
In this small car

Her job requires
Driving day and night
Slippy roads of island clay
Pot holes, in lanes and roads
Torrential rain, hot sun
She needed a car with fun

Now for her auto quest
She searched long and far
And most of the used rigs
She found out to be
To her very sad dismay
Were silver or grey

She needed a bright color
To help make her day
Yellow, Orange, Red
Bright Blue or Green
Not that silvery grey
More money she'll pay

Our story ends soon
As a very bright red
Sunroof, Volkswagen Jetta
Has stolen her heart
Power windows, custom air
It matches her bright red hair

Oh those car payments
They are part of love
She has found a rig
One not of silver or grey
Look for that flowing
Bright red head of hair
See her smile on the fly
As Dorrie races on by

Found a Penny

Went to the store
To buy her a gift
A special present
That she had wished

I went to the counter
With all my money
A nice gift I had bought
Just for my sweet honey

The lady said to me
You're short one cent
You've got to be kidding
And out the door I went

I stood there outside
And I looked around
I checked my pockets
Not penny I found

So I said, "Hey buddy!
Can you lend me a penny?"
He said that he would
If he only had any

I asked another fellow,
"Sir, do you have a cent?"
He shrugged his shoulders
And away he went

The tears rolled down
From my eyes to my cheek
They fell down on my foot
But there lay on the street

That badly needed penny
This was all I was looking for
I stood there grinning
Then headed back to the store

The Buy-Rite had closed
Jen had locked the door
But I said I had the penny
The one I was short before

She said she was sorry
But rules are rules
Away I went from the store
Feeling like such a fool

Went to sit in my car
About to drive back home
The car wouldn't start
I sat in the parking lot alone

But I had found that
Elusive lucky penny
It should bring me luck
But I didn't see any

Frankie came driving by
He busted my old car
I hope it stays running
Do you have to drive far?

I headed back home
To see my sweet honey
Without that perfect gift
But with plenty of money

Then I hit a skunk
Knocking out a light
This was the making
Of not a good night

She met me at the door
With a smile on her face
Then, "You smell like a skunk
Get away from this place!"

But, but I do have a gift
I have it right here honey
Holding out my hand
Was my lucky penny money

Oh leave this house now
You are cheap and do stink
And on this relationship
I'll need time to think

I had sent him to Buy-Rite
For a gift I did adore
And all that I got was
A skunk standing at the door

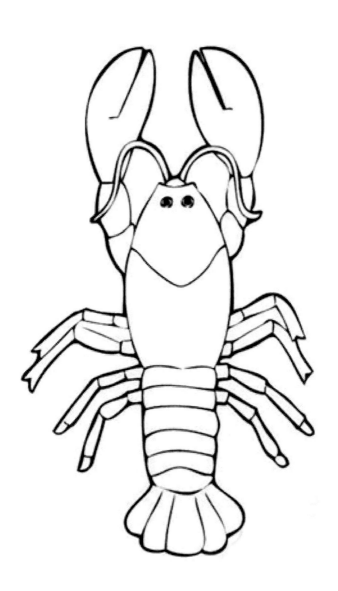

Lobster on a Plane

Well, the trip back was uneventful until Lester the Lobster managed to break free from his travel box (someone in security had dropped it on the concrete floor, breaking a corner). A strange scrabbling sound was heard from the overhead luggage bin, then the door popped open, and Lester dove for the drinks cart, and started ripping open pretzel packages and dumping them into the water jug, until it had enough salt so he could get in and get a breath of seawater.

Most of the passengers missed this activity, being distracted by screaming stewardesses and Torontonians scrambling to get on top of their seats (and banging their heads into the luggage bins). Fortunately, a young man from Murray River saw what was happening, and walked up, pocketed a few wee bottles of scotch, grabbed Lester and smashed his skull. He then shuffled back to his seat muttering something unflattering about 'folk from away'

Bob Pickering

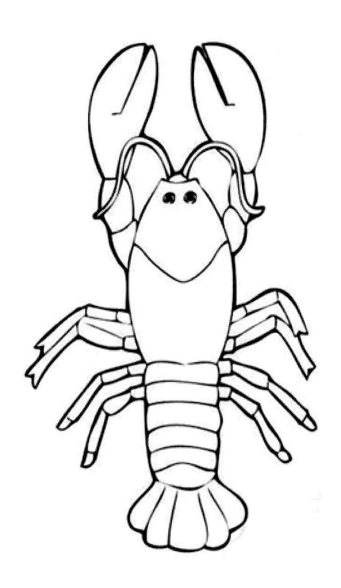

Salt Water Sam   8

Salt water Sam
Is a hell of a man?
Doing the best he can

Time to trim the tree
The flag you can't see
A job for Sam and me

We're fishermen on a boat
To climb this tree, no hope
We have no ladder or rope

Leslie Stewart: Go'Way!

Sam's afraid he might fall
This troubled tree is very tall
But some braches are small

It would be best to use a chainsaw
This tree was planted my our pa
In his vision of us he never saw

Two full grown men of the sea
Afraid to climb his planted tree
But it was Sam said it to me

He was afraid he might fall
And this old tree was very tall
He could see the ground that's all

Let's do the cutting at night
With the chainsaw use a light
Fasten it to the bar real tight

He's my brother what a plan
I wish I was as smart as Sam
We'll cut tonight if we can

The logic is this you see
At night it's better to cut a tree
And you won't be afraid like me

If you can't see the ground
You're not afraid to fall down
And that my friend is profound

Sealed with a Pie

It was on a Wednesday
When Fisheries Minster
Our, Honourable Gail Shea
Got smacked in the face
With a cream pie, I say

An American lady responsible
For this cowardly display
Rushed from the audience
And pied poor Gail Shea

Some of you laughed?
Others sat in dismay
To think a seal loving
Person, did act this way

She did it just for them
The seals that can't speak
She attack a helpless lady
As a mugger on the street

She should be banished
To live on a Atlantic ice flow
She could live with the seals
Her cousins she would know

When she is stranded there alone
Out in the Gulf on that cold ice
She'll remember throwing a pie
In Gail's face wasn't very nice

Trim for a King

Barber, barber, give me a trim
I want to look just like him
Take this picture of this guy
With your scissors will you try?
All the ladies are mad for him
After this cut, I'm off to the gym
Add some color make it black
Do a good job; I'll be back
Make a big wave on my head
The ladies will surf me in bed
Add some oil; make it shine
Really cool haircut of mine
Sideburns long devil's fork
They'll not be calling me a pork
I'll lose a few pounds or two
Are you just about through?
Great job: This is the new me
I'll be the one the chicks see
Thanks Sheldon, you the man
You did the best job you can
It's up to me to do all the rest
Wish I had a bra for my breast
Makes no matter, I'm on the prow!
Where's the babe from Montague now?

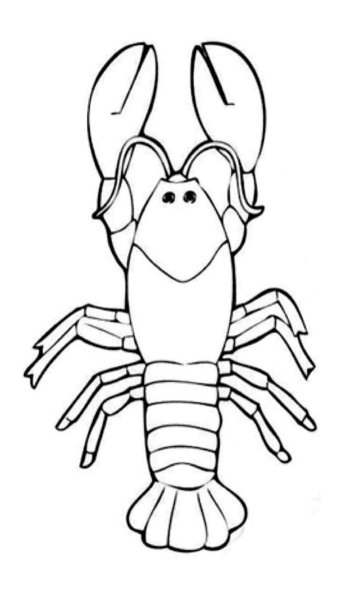